Praise for Stephan Silich's
"the silence between what i think and what i say"

"Brilliant, timeless, contemplative and emotionally intelligent insights into the human condition. Two thumbs way up!"
– Paul Kuhn

"Silich bares his soul in his work. I see myself, my mom, my life in his words. That's how you know it's good, when it takes on a life of it's own."
– Linda P. Kester

"In that familiar silence between thought and speech, Stephan Silich illuminates a world of joy, sorrow, love, loss and life. Read his poetry to reveal the depths of your own silences through remarkable words and images of this gifted poet."
– Susan Taylor

"Stephan Silich's collection of poetry is a wonderful expression of emotions which are very personal but to which we can all relate. It allows us as readers to reflect, to acknowledge dreams and hopes and to contemplate our own failures and achievements. Strongly recommend this poet's writing!"
– Marta Lee

"There is so much emotion in his thoughtful writing that many times he evokes joy, tears, and such strong love. Beautiful book filled with love."
– Marion Pisani

I bought this book based on the title and cover photo, but was speechless after reading it in its entirety through the night. The largeness of the emotion is something I have never experienced before especially reading a male poet. The words seem almost motherly in a sense. I found the entire book disarmingly feminine with a voice so gently tender and overwhelmingly seductive and alluring - in a literary and life sense. The author has a pure gift of which I have never seen before and I thank him for so bravely opening up to this sad and confused world. Stephan's words saved me.
– Karyn Lombardo

From the dedication throughout the collection, I was mesmerized by the author's perspective and ability to communicate it through depth, warmth and affection. It will take a few re-reads to really tap into this collection, but I found it profoundly impactful on first read.
– Gerry Murphy

Each morning I turn to a random page in my new treasure. I realize that at once the sweetest of voices has made its way to print. Stephan's poetry has helped me begin yet another day otherwise taken for granted.
– Rita Calvo

The book is exquisite in every aspect, from its heartfelt content to its perfect presentation. Truly a work of art!
– Dr Terri Prendergast

I really enjoyed this collection of poetry and actually found it hard to read only one poem a day and hence finished the book in one day. I am thankful for the author's allowing me a glimpse into his heart and soul. What really strikes me most about the author besides his love for his family, is his humility. What a precious gift so few people learn in life.
– Alex Cano

Also by Stephan Silich

the silence between what i think and what i say

tonight
will
be
the
longest
night
of
them
all

stephan silich

BROOKLYN
WRITERS PRESS

All rights reserved.
Published in New York City by the Brooklyn Writers Press,
an imprint of the Brooklyn Writers Project, LLC.

www.brooklynwriterspress.com

TITLE: Tonight Will Be The Longest Night of Them All

ISBN: 978-0-9896037-4-4 (e-book)
ISBN: 978-0-9896037-5-1 (paperback)
ISBN: 978-1-7340973-4-4 (hardback)

Library of Congress Catalog Card Number: 2019914284

1st Edition

Cover photograph by Stephan Silich
Cover design by Andrej Rudolf Semnic

for my daughters, emma and mia.
my brother, robert.
my parents, robert and dianne.

as always, this is for you.

"A thing of beauty will never pass into nothingness."

- Bench Plaque, Central Park, New York

contents

the eternal present
(2008)

the secret
is being aware
that life is the eternal present.

most jobs and careers
professionalize you
by shearing away all
your outside interests and dedications.

be strong enough
not to allow that to happen,
and brave enough to leave it behind
and choose another direction.

dedicate your soul to silence.

try and survive the first truth.

turn the ordinary into something rare.

don't care to appear profound.

sing the songs of life with kindness.

stay unburdened by the whispered sorrows of youth.

recite the meditations of your heart.

keep the words simple and unadorned
even when surrounded by desolation.

surrender to it all and tear it all apart
so that whatever waits in the shadows,
whether treasures or horror,
can openly be discovered.

be generously demonstrative to the people you love.

and hold on to the remembrance
that there may still be
one sweet moment left for you.

an instant

you sometimes
have only an instant
to fall in love
with the passerby
you may never see again.

it can be haunting
but beautiful,
for the simple fact
that you have
only a small chance
and a brief moment
to recognize
a little piece
of a person's soul.

much the same way
you capture a glimpse
of a person's life
in 1/100th of a second
with a photograph.

.

new york city

seek out the city's skyline
to get your bearings,
and anchor yourself
in the place
where you'll find
both the comfort of her womb
and the majesty of her open sky.

capacity

every night
while you sleep,
i caress your faces
out of a devotion
i cannot yet name.

knowing you are breathing
in the next room,
under the same roof,
is enough.

i touch your cheeks
and your foreheads,
your chins
and your noses,
your ears
and your eyebrows,
as time dissolves
in these small gestures
of grace and beauty.

i am crushed daily
by the boundless immensity
of the sacred tenderness
i have for you
two little ladies.

this adoration
grows by the minute,
unbending and radiating,

a testament
to the enormity of my love
and the astonishing
capacity of the human heart.

truth

keep focused
on the image of
quiet tirelessness,
noncompetitive strength,
and the bohemian musings
of those pillars of
truth and decency:

the quiet buddha
and the howling bukowski.

my languid escape

i sit by myself
for hours
under the clear night sky.

at the furthest reaches
of my solitude,
i continue
to write these words
on small pieces of paper.

before this,
i died 1,000 times
in 1,000 different ways,

but i plead with my beating heart:

"don't fail me now,"

for i still long for that someone
who will burn the sorrow from my eyes.

time and death

you don't know
how i'm feeling
or what i'm feeling...

if i look at my watch,
i may be noting
the time of death
and not necessarily the time of day,

so please remember that.

and remember that
all the people we love
will die
and some
will die before you.

hold on to that.

let it unburden
everything else
that is just not important.

50 things i've learned in 50 years

1. the love you leave behind is all that matters.

2. winning is actually the unforgiving monster that never allows you to rest. it's not what it seems and it's not worth it. that being said, losing doesn't make you a better person, but it does make you a person.

3. the best dreams begin in the morning, after you open your eyes.

4. it's almost always about the money, and that's one of the saddest things in the world that you will ever realize.

5. keep your friends close, as close as you can. keep your enemies away, as far away as possible. don't follow that other saying. it's simply not true.

6. if you love completely and honestly, there will always be a small sorrow in your heart.

7. make sure your faults add to, rather than subtract from, the sum of your achievements.

8. lying seems to be a manifestation of being afraid of something. don't be afraid. be brave and be truthful.

9. don't think something better is around the corner, that's a myth. appreciate what you have and stop the wandering eye. it's all right in front of you.

10. don't compromise on love because, at some point, what you really want will find its way to the surface.

11. it's the things you don't do in life, not the things you do, that should create the regret.

12. the truth will slip out when we stumble, when we make mistakes, and when we have accidents.

13. grief is the price we pay for love.

14. you have to live apart to know that you are not alone.

15. if you can't be their first love, then be their last, because the last first kiss is just as important

16. with absolute attention and absolute relaxation is how you should approach your work and your life.

17. love more each day and remember it's always: "more than yesterday and less than tomorrow."

18. great photographs should be on the quiet side because you are, in essence, catching the element of time.

19. try to be a good person, not great, just good, in a world that for the most part is either cold, hostile, or indifferent. all you can do is put forth the daily effort.

20. many of us despair over the things we want in life and the things we didn't get, but the key is still having the desire to celebrate what you already have.

21. most people are yearning for something more, something intimate, something lasting, but are afraid of realizing that it's attainable. everything you want is right outside your door.

22. many people need their victories, like cutting in front of you while driving or while standing in line to board a plane. give it to them because life has failed them, but more importantly, they have failed life.

23. the vulgar pursuit of riches always excludes art and literature, and it contributes absolutely nothing to society.

24. stay emotional because your emotions dictate what's important to you.

25. remember, we lose everything in the end, but also realize that we don't actually lose anything at all.

26. quitting, or rather walking away, is always an honorable option, under the right circumstances.

27. forget the saying that whatever doesn't kill you makes you stronger. sometimes what doesn't kill you should have. and sometimes what doesn't

kill you leaves you permanently scarred. it's how you walk through the fire that makes the difference.

28. it's the in-between moments that count the most.

29. your silence will be the most eloquent thing about you.

30. not every man dreams himself a king.

31. decency is necessary for all.

32. what is often best in people seldom has a chance to show itself. look closely for it; it's there.

33. don't let your humanness catch them by surprise.

34. between night and nothingness, choose night.

35. ignore the desperate self-consciousness of the overly ambitious.

36. how you treat people who can do nothing for you is most important.

37. privacy is the only true kindness of the soul.

38. tell that one person, unreservedly, of your hopes unrealized and your promises unfulfilled. withhold nothing.

39. don't respond to the forced graciousness of others.

40. try not to lose anyone that carries your history.

41. keep a devotion for books and a quiet life. stay rich in inward ways.

42. vanish and resurrect yourself if you have to.

43. stay indifferent to criticism but also to praise.

44. give yourself wholeheartedly to life's mysteriousness.

45. don't miss the pure beauty that is right in front of you.

46. it's always the moment just before.

47. sometimes a single moment is more important than an entire life story.

48. every once in a while a hand is extended; reach for it.

49. the big decisions in life are the ones that turn out to have the least impact on life as a whole. it's the small, seemingly insignificant ones, that make the difference.

50. and remember poets are never alone, right?

the exquisite sleep

do you remember that night
in the upstairs bedroom:

half-opened shutters,
half-moonlight,
the moment right after…

followed by the exquisite sleep
of your naked body
that i loved
and awoke to
on sunday mornings.

those same mornings
my eyelids always approved of,
welcoming the new day
with your hair
across the pillow?

that was enough.

resistant

these neighborhood stores,
garden cafés,
and cobblestone streets
make up the
tender details
so enduringly rarified
in the everyday life
of this city
that dissolves
some of the anonymity
of our lives
and continually reminds us
that love is found in these places
and that love is always resistant
to the passage of time.

the soho house

she invited me to the soho house
for a movie premiere.

she was a founding member and wanted to treat me to a rare night out since
anyone who knows me knows how much i like that old quote by bukowski:
"i don't hate people, i just seem to feel better when they're not around."

they checked my name on the guest list
and told me to go to the 6th floor.

i got off the elevator and she was waiting at the bar
with a bottle of wine.

she told me to grab 2 glasses and the bucket of ice.

we headed down to the 5th floor's private screening room, which seats about
20 on oversized leather chairs, with ambient music and soft lighting.

we drank and ate and lounged in languid splendor.

afterward,
we headed to another floor and ordered more drinks and food.

i was introduced to a documentary filmmaker,
and he asked if we would join him at the bar
because his ex was there and she kept bumping into him
and throwing ice cubes at him.

i asked if he meant his ex-wife and he said:

"no, just the mother of my second child."

he said the last time he saw her was a few months ago. they were living
together in little italy, and he told her he couldn't take it anymore and was
leaving her.

she grabbed a kitchen knife and chased him down the street, past the old
couples sitting on nearby park benches, screaming:

"if i can't have you, no one else will."

i smiled and said:

"now that's love."

he laughed and said:

"it's the only kind worth living for."

he told us he was going over to talk to her.
i said it was nice meeting him and he said the same.

he walked away smiling,
and i returned to my wine.

urgency

find inspiration in the urgency of existence

and remember

that you cut the wood

that made these doors

that lead to these rooms

that hold your family

and this is your meditation on love

and the mark of a virtuous

and reverent life.

songs from a fire escape

the wind off the hudson
filtered through the air
and through these
downtown buildings
as she stepped out
onto the fire escape,
a backdrop of laundry
hanging low over the railing,
a vase of summer flowers,
and a white lamp with a white shade
sitting on the steps
alongside colored lanterns.

there was another light above her head,
which swayed with the breeze,
casting her in light and shadow
as she sang melancholy fragments
about life and love.

we stood there together,
arm in arm,
as witnesses
to the splendid randomness
of this new york moment.

we stood there together
as the security guard yelled at everyone
not to block the exit.

we stood there together
as the elderly man sat alone,
his head slightly lowered.

and we stood there together
as the empire state
watched in the distance,
and we watched the couple
in the nearby hotel window
embrace as true lovers do.

squint

a city's character
is rooted in the grain
of everyday life
by the people
that actually live here
and sleep here
under the lights of buildings
that look like stars
if you squint hard enough.

even if just for tonight

stick around long enough,
and something beautiful
will be taken away from you.

stick around longer still,
and something more beautiful
will be taken away from you.

and stick around until the very end,
and everything will be taken away from you.

yet, knowing all this,
would you do it over again?

of course you would.

even if for one night,
it would be well worth it.

written by emma, 5 years old
(father's day, june 2018)

1) <u>my dad is:</u> *cool*
2) <u>he likes:</u> *going in the pool with me*
3) <u>he always:</u> *loves me*
4) <u>the best thing about my dad is:</u> *he sleeps and cuddles with me.*

and with this
i am rendered
unutterably moved
by my children's nobility,
because these words alone

demolish empires,

destroy kings,

and make grown men weep.

right

always do the right hard things,
rather than the easy wrong things.

it will give you just the right amount
of courage and devotion
for the moment
your reach exceeds your grasp.

a downtown night

up four flights to her apartment
on the corner of prince and thompson.

we shared a bottle of wine
on an 80-degree summer night
as slivers of moonlight
filtered through the handmade curtains.

we lay there sharing stories
about the last few years
and the present state of our lives.

at around 1 o'clock,
i made my way down the stairs,
looked out the 2nd floor window,
and noticed a group of people
sitting on the balcony,
under a dark green umbrella,
surrounded by candlelight,
food,
drinks,
laughter,
and friendship.

it was a beautiful night indeed.

sunset

the light from the hudson
reflects warmly
off the surrounding buildings
as you stand in front of me.

i barely notice the glorious sunset
over your shoulder.

without a trace

i will never tell you
how difficult
my days
and weeks
and years
have actually been
because i'm hoping
that some of these words
reach someone
somewhere
and help them push past
the ache of despair

and become beautiful again,
without showing
any trace of having worked at it.

completely content

i daydream.
i cry when i feel like crying.
i tell my parents i love them.
i'm best friends with my brother.
i had a beautiful childhood.
i write these words when i want.
i paint and draw with my daughters.
i walk them to school every morning.
i build my own furniture.
i take pictures of what i love.
and all my heroes are artists.
so i may not be a man
by today's definition.

i try to be effortlessly kind,
as my mom taught me,
but i do punch back if punched first,
as my dad taught me.
and sometimes i punch first, if necessary,
so i actually may still be a man.

i do know that i am completely content,
and i know for sure:

that nothing breaks like the heart.

additional thoughts

sit with those sitting alone.

look for the good.

work quietly with a small amount of attention.

cherish the thinking life.

never really fit in.

notice everything.

allow for moments of pure soaring beauty.

have unyielding compassion.

remember the dignity of language.

memorize where your arms go when hugging your children.

stay unapologetically earnest.

feel the wetness of every tear.

retain the elusive concept of authenticity.

tell the stories of lives that many think small.

restore the opportunity to linger wordlessly.

find solace in the nowness of everywhere.

stay imperfect and incomplete.

fight the wars, not the battles.

express the depths of ordinary life.

allow yourself to stay vividly present.

and know when to walk away from it all.

birthday

sometimes
it's nice
just realizing
that someone you know
was born today.

life's reply

it's late at night,
but i still believe there's time
to get some of this down on paper,
because it's the struggle,
which is the actual victory,
that keeps the light in our eyes.

my thoughts drift
to the wise peasant,
the good and decent man,
with so much to vote against,
but not much to vote for,
who still
stares into the evening sky
and awaits the expectation
of life's monumentally elegant reply.

jazz
(may 26, 2001)

last night
i went to see the shirley horn trio
at the blue note jazz club
in greenwich village.

it was a quiet, rainy night,
and i didn't know much
about jazz or shirley horn,
but i was willing
to give it a shot
on the invitation
from my brother,
who, by the way,
is always right
about music
and just about everything else in life.

after
the introduction,
there was silence.

after the silence,
there was music.

it was
a bit melancholic,
but it instantly reminded
me of her
and how every time
i went to her house
the same kind of music
was languidly playing
on her father's stereo.

he worked for a local radio station
and ran the sunday afternoon jazz show.

i loved hearing the music,
standing in her living room,
waiting for her to come down the stairs
looking beautiful, as she always did.

it was also the kind of music
i loved hearing

on a rainy new york night
sitting next to my brother
and thinking of her.

my thoughts were mostly of how she would
come home from work at 2:30 in the morning,
take a long hot shower,
and then ask me to take the mattress
from the upstairs bedroom
and put it
in front of the fireplace.

we would lie there,
drink wine,
and fall asleep.

we slept close
and her body was always warm.

she had this habit of
twirling her foot in tiny circles
before she fell asleep.

it is what i miss most.

and as i sat there listening to the music,
this was all i could think about,
thanks to my brother and the shirley horn trio.

children

i will hopefully
remain a child

and always
remain gentle with children,

because we are all children in the end,
when we let go of this life for the last time.

the key

remain
human
enough
while
trying
to
extinguish
the
midday
sun.

purpose

lover of the long shot.

defender of lost causes.

lucky enough
to laugh at it all.

sincere about the things
most people take lightly.

unconcerned about the things
most people take seriously.

and still wanting to give
the best hours of my day
to you alone.

the mysterious ache

great love
should leave you
slightly exhausted every day,

and it should also leave you
slightly sad every day.

it's what i refer to as
the mysterious ache.

the merits of tenderness

i walked past the restaurant
and paused to remember
our first night together.

i breathed in a bit of the air
coming from the east river
in order to save a fragment
of the place you made so memorable.

i'll walk home
alongside these grey buildings
full of people unimaginably alone,
and i'll suppress
the incoherence of my heart,
but it will illuminate
the human condition,
the delirium of spirit,
and the unfailing merits of tenderness.

my first poem

i wrote
when i was 13
for a girl who was 14
who had long blonde hair
and bright blue eyes.

i wrote it
on white loose-leaf paper,
folding it into thirds and
putting it in an envelope
with her name on the front in all capitals.

(maybe this is why i write now in all lowercase.)

i decided to give it to her
on a friday night
at the local skating rink.

she was
with a bunch of friends,
mostly guys i didn't know
but recognized from other schools.

i walked over
and handed her the poem:

"this is for you.
i wrote this for you.
i hope you like it."

"oh, thanks," she said
and turned back to her friends.

i watched her open it
and read it without expression.

she handed it to
an ugly-faced kid with a gold earring
and brown leather jacket.

he read it
and laughed.

he handed it to the next kid.
he laughed.

their laughter
trembled through me
as they passed it
from one to the next.

i stared as they stared,
and i was ready
if it turned into a fight.

i kept staring
until they turned
and walked away first.

i removed my skates
and walked out.

i waited in the cold
for my mom to pick me up.
(thankfully, she was always early.)

"did you have fun?"
she asked.

"i don't think
ice-skating is for me."

"that's ok, any cute girls?"

"not anymore."

it was quiet the rest of the ride home.

i don't have a great memory,
but i remember that night well.

perhaps things that happen to you
in early life stay with you, because
i never ice-skated again,
and i never shared my writing
with anyone other than family and friends...

until now that is.

36 years later.

a glimmer of possibility

the fractured hours
of this night
bring the fragile
recovery of hope.

our timelessness
pushes through
with a subtlety
that is hard to define
and an endurance
that is a glimmer
of possibility.

we were once defeated,
but are now triumphant,
and this will be
the quiet redemption
of our unhurried happiness.

chance

everyone leaves
in the end,
if they get the chance.

you don't have to.

you can see this straight through
to the last moment.

my soul

the heartbreaking delicacy
of people and their lives
fills me
with an intimate gentleness,
season after season,
that pushes me past
the fractured smiles,
and makes every face a memory,
and everything else
impossibly exquisite,

while the magic
of everyday life
resurrects the refractions
of my soul
during the serene,
ceaseless searching
for what the gods left out.

we sleep

the sun sets
over the westside rooftops
of these weathered buildings,

and the night sky
bounces off early moonlight
as we sleep,
undisturbed,
near the open window.

and we are left
with a windswept graciousness
of what a peaceful life
could look like.

emma and the milkshake
(january 11, 2019)

spending the morning with my soon to be 6-year-old.
stopping off for lunch:

2 hot dogs,
2 french fries,
2 vanilla milkshakes.

i listened to the song overhead
with lyrics about protesting life's passage.

emma ate a few french fries
and moved closer to me,
slowly climbing on top of my lap,
half on the table and half on me.

tears started in her eyes
as she held my face close
and said:
"daddy, i'm going to miss you when you die,"
and then rested her head gently on my chest.

i nervously smiled
and said:
"i'm not going to die anytime soon, emma."

and without missing a beat
she said:
"ok, daddy. can i have another milkshake then?"

the song continued
about remaining bound by love.

we walked to the counter holding hands,
and i ordered another milkshake.

extra large.
2 straws.

the time is now

you can't repeat
the brilliance of this day.

the time is now.

you can't get back
the minutes,
the hours,
the years,
the decades.
the centuries.

this is it.

these words

my hands feel heavy as i write these words,
words that will most likely be forgotten.

but that is precisely the reason
for writing them.

they are the finest gift you
can bestow on another.

a simple recollection
of what once moved us
in that time
in that place
in that moment.

the next sunset

the early hours of morning
can sometimes seem
like an endless expanse
of uncharted territory
when you're alone
and under the covers.

yet i lie here
running my hands
through your dark hair,
which is artistically spread out
across the white cotton sheets.

i lie here
searching for those imperishable words,
which echo with reticence
and muted truth,
bearing witness to this era,

and crushing
a decade's worth of heartbreak
while deconstructing
the arrival of the next sunset.

can't forget

please
still
love
these
eyes
that
watch
the
world
and
can't
forget.

after the wine

in
the
end

after
the
wine

there
is
only
you.

sleeping & dreaming

there is no more elegant sleeper than you.

your curved body
resting on your left side,
my arms around you.

i sleep,
thanking you
for the intimate stoppage of time,
until morning
wakes me
to the realization
that i had not
stopped dreaming about you
for one single moment.

resplendent
(wall street, 2007)

no work can shame me,
no matter how useless or repetitive.

no boss can defeat me,
no matter how self-centered and untruthful.

no colleague can upset me,
no matter how deceiving and opportunistic.

no money or title, or lack thereof,
can ever make a difference.

no promotion to worry about.
no salary to define yourself by.

and so there will luckily be
no country clubs to join,
no restaurant openings to attend,
no sports car to buy,
no mistress to sleep with,
no tennis to play,
definitely no golf to play,
no watches to wear,
and no suits to be tailored.

you can demonstrate this
by the simple act of living
where the road will be too long
and the sky too vast,

by pushing forward
with intrepid
and unsung exuberance
until true love
finds you in the end,
one way or another,

and it will be more resplendent
than anything you could ever imagine.

images of you

i close my eyes
for a glimpse of you.

your silhouette
in the frame of the bathroom door.

a wide smile through
the open window.

a glance across the street
as you walk to work.

and these words,
appearing and reappearing,
as a fragile commentary on love.

a love
with its own soundtrack,
where every song
is written for us.

songs
giving voice to the eternal.

images
giving sight to the infinite.

and time
giving us this memory.

stay

stay
touchingly vulnerable
to everything around you

and give yourself time.

just a little more time
to wrap your arms around
your own
exquisitely moving portrait
of daily life.

mia and her pink balloon

watching mia,
my 3-year-old,
look at her hand,
almost knowing if she opens it,
the string will slip through.

the consequences of not holding on…
the consequences of not holding on tight enough…

beauty arrives
as we watch it float away,
soaring silently
over buildings
and monuments
and trees,
just beneath
the clouds.

i tell her
every blue sky needs a pink balloon.
as she turns to cry in my arms,
she looks back
to watch the balloon's
unforgettable brilliance
as it fades from view.

nothing

there is nothing more tender
than this moment.

a day at the psych unit

on a rainy sunday
she asked me
if i would go with her to visit her mom,
so we jumped into the car
and headed out of the city.

as it turns out,
her mom had been diagnosed with schizophrenia
and was living in a psychiatric facility by the ocean
in far rockaway, new york.

we arrived, checked in with security, and
were told to go to the recreation room.

she was sitting alone at a wooden table, waiting.

she waved us over and we made our way through the
room, passing a few residents along the way.

a man in a wheelchair grabbed my arm and asked:

"did we win the war?"

"of course we did," i said

he smiled and asked if i would talk to him.

"ok."

"can you take me outside so i can look at the ocean?" he said.

"if the weather lets up, i'll come get you."

when i finally reached the table,
i was introduced
and she gave me a huge kiss
right on the lips
and a near-suffocating hug.

we all sat down and began talking.
we sat there for 2 hours,
telling stories and laughing.

i was drinking a soda and she asked for a sip.

i slid my can over and, after a gulp, she said:

"now i know your secrets."

our eyes locked for a moment and we both smiled.

she asked for a cigarette.

i went to the in-house store
and bought her a carton.

she grabbed the box, leaped up, and ran off to the
women's bathroom.

a few others followed her,
and after a good 10 minutes,
they all came out,
each holding a few packs.

she was smiling
while folding handfuls of cash
into her pockets.

she said thank you and suggested we go outside
for a smoke.

as we headed to the elevator,
i grabbed the guy in the wheelchair
and off we went.

we reached the top floor
and made our way out to the balcony.

i wish i could say that at that moment
the sun broke and the sea illuminated,
but it pretty much stayed grey and cloudy.
and that was more than ok.

she lit up a cigarette
and took a few deep inhales
as the guy in the wheelchair stared straight ahead
and asked again, "did we win the war?"

we all just sat there,
looking at each other in silence,
the pounding ocean
in front of us.

we stayed like that for a while,
until her mom began to sing softly
in spanish.

she sang the same line over and over.

i asked her what it meant
and she translated:

"don't cry for me, for i have lost my only love,
but it will be ok."

and so i stood there,
letting this moment wash over me,

and that was my first and only
day at the psych unit.

a day i never wanted to end,
and a place i never wanted to leave.

unchanging on the edge of time

we walk through
the sleeping streets
of this old city,
over uneven cobblestones
and under drooling balconies,
which always seem to bring
afternoons of lingering intimacy.

we remain present
through our days,
once delicate and unadorned,
now unchanging on the edge of time,
navigating the stars at night
and the planets that bend between us.

class president
(january 2018)

st. ignatius loyola day nursery
pre-kindergarten
little emma
voted class president.

not sure about elections for 4-year-olds,
but with the victory
came the reward of asking the other students
to do something for her at the end of each school day,
like clean her play area or get her a glass of apple juice.

instead she asked that each child
line up before leaving for the day
and give her a kiss and a hug goodbye.

what more could i ask from her
as she tries to find her place in the world?

the yearning for simplicity
has been found in this startling moment
as the humanity of her gesture shudders through me.

with every passing day, i sense more deeply
my mother and father's hand in my life,
and the story continues...

the world in all its detail

the rarest of human experiences, those which produce
genuine awe, are right in front of us.

life can be a work of art
filled with grandeur and nostalgia
and elegance,
accessible to all,
if you let it,
because what we actually seek is already found.

having a hushed reverence
for the dignity of modest things
and the world in all its detail
certainly helps:

the smell of the breeze rising from the ocean,
the layers of sunlight through the kitchen window,
the sound of a few notes of music,
the naked back on the other side of the bed,
the clouds sailing easily into the distance,
the desserts lined up in the café display,
the faces of strangers we pass on the street,
and the laughter of children from the nearby schoolyard.

stay open to your dreams
and live in the daily masterpiece
that is you.

the way it ought to be

after all this time,
you still
make these brief moments
stretch breathlessly
toward an eternity i cannot name.

and it is in these moments,
when we retreat from the world,
that we glimpse life the way it ought to be.

what you mean to me

you fill that space
between childhood reminiscence
and grown-up reflection.

this trace of wistfulness
expands with each passing minute.

and even
our briefest moment together
means more to me
than the time spent
with others across a lifetime.

the light

a moment stirred by laughter,
a piece of forgotten music,
a true sensation of kindness,
eyes full of trust,
the slow beat of your heart on top of mine,
words whispered in the dark,
the splendid shadow of your spirit,
the beauty of your fragility,
the quietness after,
and the exquisiteness
of your face in the morning.

i will keep writing these words for you
and keep them pressed
between the pages of my youth,
marked by triumph,
inspired by courage.

with this,
i wonder what is the secret
behind the blue light of the night sky.

the riveting light
under which i kissed you for the first time.

the light that continues to illuminate
all that you are to me.

the light i look to
when the moon is rising
and the sun is resting.

the light that allows me to capture
a moment of you in a photograph.

the light that wraps around my hands
as my hands wrap around you.

and the light that provided us with grace
on that first morning
when we surrendered to each other.

a note from my father
(march 27, 2019)

received a note from my 77-year-old father
today that read:

"just thinking about you,
as i always do,
and hoping you are ok,
realizing the stress and pressure
you are under.
mom and i love you
beyond all reason
and will always do so.
we will always be here,
should you need us."

the continuous existence of my father's love
allows humanity to exhale the time gone by
and attach everything to the here and now.

thank you, dad.

i have lived for love

all i ever wanted
was to love a woman
the way men say they do
in those old forgotten songs:
instantly,
completely,
and until the day i die.

i will keep trying to
look past being haunted
in a haunting city
and walk straight into my fears,
whose boundaries
will be broken
by dreams that never end.

remember

these words
are the same
as the person who writes them,
and it's the best i can give.

but it's the most of you
that becomes the most of me.

infinite possibility
(for emma and mia, march 2019)

give me this moment
to look at you
and let me feel
what this has to offer.

let it remain
the towering breath of integrity
that we were promised.

let it allow me to love you,
meticulously and unyieldingly,

and let it lead
the silent procession of my heart
as it marches towards
the infinite possibility
that is you.

cleaning erasers and strawberry lip gloss

8th grade
st. joseph hill academy:
i was often given detention
for disruptive behavior.

as part of my "rehabilitation,"
i had to clean all the
classroom erasers
at the end of each school day.

so every day at 2 o'clock,
i would gather
the erasers
and head downstairs
to the maintenance room,
where the cleaning
machine was located.

it was a small
brown electric device
that would act as
a kind of
high-powered vacuum
and
remove all
the chalk
at once.

i did this
routine
every day, alone,
until one day
i found
the most
welcome company
waiting for me.

i walked in
and said hello.

she smiled,
curled her hair
behind one ear,

and said hi.

i stood next to her
and waited my turn.

i stared at her
blue and grey checkered
school-issued uniform.

she was also wearing a navy sweater,
and i imagined
the wool being softer than it looked.

when she finished her erasers,
she turned to me
and said,
"i'll see you tomorrow?"
"2 o'clock!"
"don't be late."

the next day couldn't come fast enough.
i headed down with my erasers at 1:59 p.m.
on the way, i feverishly smacked the
erasers against each other
and the walls
to get rid of all the chalk.

this way,
i could save some time,
as i figured
every minute counts.

when i got there,
she was waiting.

we didn't speak at all
but immediately started kissing,
as fast and as awkwardly
as two 13-year-olds could.

the strawberry flavor
of her lip gloss
instantly burst
inside my mouth.

we kissed until
just before
the bell rang,
ending the school day.

we ran back to our classes,
returned the erasers,
and headed home.

the next day,
same time,
same thing.

this went on for about two months
and no one was the wiser.

the erasers
were always returned clean,
we always made it to our classes
before the 2:30 p.m. bell,
and i was always treated
to a different flavor lip gloss:

first strawberry,
then watermelon,

then cherry,
then strawberry again.

there was simply
no better way to serve detention,
and it was a terrific way
to spend the last minutes
of each school day.

and as i write this,
decades later,
i can close my eyes
and still taste that strawberry.

so thank you
to whatever gods are responsible
for these small miracles of youth.

question #1

will
the
weight
of
our
ashes
equal
the
weight
of
our
birth
?

the way we choose

today
i just want to sit still,
very still,
and think about
the time lost to waiting
and the graceful recognition
of the uncertainty
for how much is left.

give me patience and restraint
and let me
affirm life,
despite everything.

give me some time
this evening,
if only
so we can keep an eye
on human frailty
with a stillness
and a depth of feeling
that no one
will ever be able
to take away from us.

peaceful perfection

from my bedroom,
i hear the prayers in the cathedral,
and i'm reminded that
i never have to travel far
to find inspiration.

it is always
in these moments,
in these miraculous nights,
ever ascendant,
which remain in my thoughts
and in a 1,000 new york windows
that change over time
like the faces of lovers.

i will continue to write
love's aria
even though
i know a lifetime
will be needed to remember you.

our eyes need rest
because we are left with
the lushness of love
unfolding upon us,
casting light instead of shadow.

and thankfully,
we are left with
the peaceful perfection
of waking up together.

never

you never have all the time
in the world.

it's that simple.

basquiat died at 28,
keats 25,
van gogh 37,
kerouac 47,
modigliani 35,
oscar wilde 46,
caravaggio 37,
franz kafka 40,
jackson pollack 44,
thoreau 44,
egon schiele 28,
rimbaud 37,
vermeer 43,
sylvia plath 30
raphael 37,
edgar allan poe 40,

and let's not forget
mozart at 35,
bob marley 36,
john lennon 40,
jim morrison 27,
billie holiday 44,
jimi hendrix 27,
freddy mercury 45,
marvin gaye 44,
hank williams 29
and elvis presley 42.

the faces will be forgotten,
but the eyes will be remembered.

so grasp this life,
make it inseparable
from your dreams,

and the fine-grained
art of every day
will be yours.

triumph bonneville

took the bike out today
and headed to the ocean.

along the coast
i drove,
with no helmet,
as the wind rose slowly
off the atlantic.

i passed
the girls walking,
the surfers waiting,
and the fishermen dreaming.

it's tough sometimes
to find meaning
in this life,
but this was pretty close.

the unavoidable smiles,
the impermanence of the allure,
and how time no longer
weighed on me
as it once had.

i reached the end of the road
and started my turnaround
when i noticed
a man sitting alone
under a single palm tree.

he had a cigarette in his hand,
deep lines in his face,
and from what i could make out,
tears in his eyes.

i looked at him
and instead of turning away
as i'd expected,
he looked directly at me
and nodded.

i nodded back

and marked
the moment
quietly.

i pushed it
into 2nd gear,
then 3rd,
checked the mirror,
and caught a glimpse of him
taking a long drag
on his cigarette
as he closed his eyes,
tilting his head
slightly toward the heavens.

it was then
that i noticed
the great courage
seeping through
every pore of his face.

i got the bike up to 60
then 70
then 80
and never looked back.

stages of grief and love

what to make
of these defined
stages of grief:
denial,
anger,
bargaining,
depression,
and acceptance.

or…

are these actually
the stages of love:
denial,
anger,
bargaining,
depression,
and acceptance?

i still believe

love is the noblest
of all causes,
and i still believe
that my last words to you
will never be spoken,
because i think of you
the exact same way
i always have
since that august night.

and i still believe
your eyes
give tired men hope.

and i still believe
everything changes
in the morning.

and i still believe
you never need room to breathe
when in the arms of another.

and i still believe
i knew you my whole life,
because you were always in my dreams.

and i do wish the end
was my beginning,
because i've experienced enough
to know that
our beginning was my end.

an aura of destiny

the map of your heart
is written
in the language
of the city you live in.

and these patterns of existence
will add a hint of destiny
to our enduring love,

and they will sing
a song for us tonight.

i am quite sure of this.

privilege

the body aches.
the mind forgets.
the heart beats slower.
the soul grows restful.

and as the final farewell approaches,
i speak to you for the last time:
to you, who cannot hear me,
to you, who cannot speak to me.

what will the last line
of my obituary read?

perhaps this:
he discovered the secret of life
was contained in one simple phrase:
growing old with you
would be an absolute privilege.

at certain hours

at certain hours of the morning,
i feel as if everything i've done
will be buried under the dust of time,
but then i remember
the elegance of days gone by.

and in the evening,
the disenchantment will dissipate;
it usually does.

and the winds of fortune
will rise,
even if ever so slightly.

is she ok?
(november, 2018)

went to central park
with my 5 and 3-year-old,
the playground on 72nd and 5th.
after an hour or so
on the swings and slides,
my 5-year-old, emma,
joined two other girls
on a rubber tire,
and i watched
as they laughed
and spun around and around.

i noticed emma every now and then
looking at the girl opposite her,
who wore a pink jacket and pink bow in her hair.
she looked like she had down syndrome.

emma would slow the spinning tire
by dragging her feet on the ground,
and then she would gently
put her hand on the girl's back
and ask, "are you having fun?
do you like it?"

after some time,
we walked to get a few hot dogs.
emma had tears in her eyes and i asked
if she was ok.
she said, "daddy, something happened to the girl.
i think she fell and hurt her face.
she's not ok'"

i said "no, no, emma. she's ok. she was born
that way. she's ok. she's playing in the park
and having fun. she's fine."

'i'm really worried, daddy.
i don't think she's ok".

this back and forth went on
for about 10 minutes

until she became distracted
with the hot dog and some vanilla ice cream.
i forgot about it also, until later that night,
after i gave them a bath,
put on their pajamas,
brushed their teeth,
read a story,
and put them to bed.

as they slept in the next room,
i remembered today.

and i write these words now, for her only,
because it's her words that provide
the consolation for this world
in each and every letter.

i don't have sufficient understanding
of what really goes on in the hearts
and souls of children,
especially children driven by pure instinct
in their pursuit of beauty in a notably
unbeautiful time,

but i do know that
the graceful and dignified feeling
of being their father is the most
profoundly humanizing,
inimitable, indelible,
and eloquent thing on earth
that simply leaves me gasping every night.

the urgent need

have conversations that matter.

don't talk about the weather or traffic.

be honest
in a way that is delivered
warmly and encouragingly.

have manners that speak for themselves.

when loved,
return that love
in equal measure.

things essentially
fall into two categories:
those that are life-enhancing
and those that are life-diminishing.

remember the former
and forget the rest.

look up every now and then
and follow the sun moving
from one wall to the next,
lovingly delaying the moment
when the lights need to be turned on.

this is your constant reminder
to experience intensely,
even if for a short period of time.

we age alongside the words we read,
and we will be dead
for much longer than we are alive.

in all probability,
we will be forgotten by most,
but remembered by that which
we manage to leave behind.

at first glance

it begins with silence.
it ends with a kiss.

where are you?

the used cigarette
staring up at me
from the rain-filled street,
the rusty bicycle
leaning against
the newly planted tree,
the empty wine bottle
stretched out on the beach.

but where are you?

you were the one
who captured more in a single word
than most capture in a lifetime.

you were the one
who portrayed humanity
in a fleeting moment,
rather than worrying
about a flawless performance.

i looked for you today
but couldn't find you.

where are you?

dreams desperate

dreams desperate unfold on stars shining
and i weep for your return.

bloom

hemingway blew his brains out.
millay drank herself to death,
as did kerouac.
basquiat did it with heroin.
pollack wrapped his car around a tree.

and let's not forget
rembrandt,
van gogh,
gauguin,
mozart,
bach,
beethoven—
all died penniless.

i think about them
as i walk along tree-lined streets,
listening to the train's screeching wheels,
and waiting for a little luck to come my way,
because i'm all too aware
of life's insinuated elegance
and indifference.

but with each death,
1,000 flowers bloom,
and eternity trembles
like the wings of a hummingbird.

yawn

i expected
an earlier exit,
but now i get to
stare at the palms
reaching upward
and watch boats
pass under cement bridges.

this is a good day.
no gunfire in the streets tonight,
and time yawning ahead
with new dreams, dreaming.

with this
upon me,
i pull the shades,
stretch out,
and realize
this is all more peaceful
than i could ever have imagined.

the early parts of morning

i watch an old man
with wild grey hair
and a face of history
sitting in a blue car.

our eyes meet
and i wonder if we've
seen each other before,
in a café perhaps,
or on a street corner.

for a brief moment,
i think we're both aware
of how humanity
continues to fail us,
in so many different ways.

he eventually
drives off
and i return
to my small room
where i lie in bed
reading words
that continue
to radiate with reverence
and light a new day.

i listen to mozart
playing down the hall,
close the book,
and dream
into the
early parts
of morning
when the clouds
will testify
that all is ok.

this unblinking moment

i endured the centuries
and survived the tears of mountains
to reach this unblinking moment.

our windows
have been opened,
and i imagine
our kisses torching the air
until i return home
and stare at the old rug,
in the old room,
where love once died,
well aware
of the passing of time
while letting absolute aloneness unfold
and yet waking every day
and still deciding to continue.

a short story
about a day i never recovered from

when i was in high school, 16 years old, i was with my parents driving my brother to college to start his pre-med program at georgetown in washington, dc.

i was in the first car with my father; he was driving. i was in the passenger seat. behind us, in another car, was my brother, mother, and grandmother. a blue bmw passed us on the right and pulled in front as we drove south on i-95.

the husband was driving, the wife was next to him, and they had 2 small girls sitting in the back playing with their dolls. we would later find out they were 7 and 5 years old. they waved to us as they drove past.

then, in an instant, a tire from an 18-wheel truck driving in the opposite direction came off, bounced into our lane, and hit them directly on the roof of the passenger side. immediately, blood covered the entire back window.

the car somehow made it to the shoulder of the road. my father pulled over behind them and my mother behind us.

the husband got out and walked straight into the middle of the highway. my father was able to grab him and gently guide him off the road.

i ran up to the passenger side and opened the door. i froze. the woman, a young wife and mother, had been decapitated. her 2 little girls were in the backseat with blood everywhere and screaming: "you killed my mommy!" "why did you kill my mommy?" "what did you do?" "why did you hurt her?"

i was confused and nauseous until i realized we didn't cause this, that it was the tire from the truck, not us. the girls were in distress and shock. i had no idea what to do.

i would love to say that i was this brave 16-year-old boy who jumped right in, but i don't remember it that way. i couldn't move. i stood there in silence and did nothing. my brother came up behind me and put a jacket over the bottom half of the woman. my mom, a pediatric nurse, climbed into the back and pulled the girls out.

my grandmother, also a nurse, sat them down, hugged them, and helped my mom clean the blood and body parts off their dresses. they asked for their dolls, so i ran back to the car and picked them up, only to find pieces of skull, brains, and an eyeball on the middle seat. i grabbed the dolls, held my breath, and closed the door. my mom took a pair of scissors and cut the dolls' hair, which was matted with blood. she handed them to the girls. they kissed their dolls, crying and rocking back and forth over and over again.

after the police and ambulances arrived, we spent the next few hours at the police station making statements until we were able to continue on our way.

i remember saying that i never wanted to see anything like that again and that's why i didn't want to be a doctor. my brother said that's exactly why he wanted to be a doctor—so he could be involved in those things and fix whatever he possibly could. so he went right; i went left. he became a plastic and reconstructive surgeon, and i went off to law school. my brother spent many years studying and then working diligently and patiently fixing and healing burn victims, cancer patients, accident survivors, children severely bitten by dogs, broken noses, cheek bones, lacerated faces and hands, chins and eyebrows, severed fingers, and much more too numerous to name. law school for me was disappointing on many levels, but i finished, graduated, and turned to writing.

haltingly, i faced my own mortality at a younger age than many, so i looked to the ancient philosophers, the long dead artists, the classic authors, and the aging musicians for answers i hoped i would find.

and so i waited many years before bringing children into this world. but with a little beauty and mystery and nature, and despite the uncertainty, and despite the despair, i joined this strange ceremony of life. i now spend most of my time writing as much as i can, so i'm known more fully while alive, and perhaps brought to mind once in a while, when i'm gone.

the weight of what's recalled and recollected and the simple art of walking my daughters to school, now the same ages as the girls in the car, haunts me with optimism and anguish.

to see this death, smell this death, hear this death, at age 16, has shaped my life in ways i am just now fully realizing.

the acceptance of my death and the death of everyone i love, has led to an understanding of life's fragility and has guided me for the last 34 years.

let me take this story a little further, let me take our history a little further, and let me catch my breath underneath this limitless and unbounded parental love.

all i ask is for a few more summers
and christmases
and birthdays.

hope

there is always hope behind the brushstrokes.

and this reminds me of a quote by a painter i read about
or maybe dreamed about.

when asked what was the deepest reason
for becoming an artist,

he replied:

"because i am heartbroken."

and i ask
of no one in particular:

"could there ever be
 a better reason than this?"

broken music

the bulls are victorious in spain
as i listen
to the gospel singer near the port authority.

love is the most often used word in suicide notes
as i listen
to the blind guitarist in times square.

attention should be given to something that doesn't
require it
as i listen
to the young girl play piano on 14th street.

men will die bent over vegetable gardens
as i listen
to the jazz band at grand central.

and a little flower grows through the cement cracks
as i listen
to the old man play violin on 125th street.

the final collapse

will my heart remain unfinished?

will the sun rise again?

will the world grow quieter?

will your touch
stay etched in my flesh?

will thoughts of you drip out
in unmeasured doses?

will you continue to echo
through the songs of poets?

will your words wait for me
until night falls?

will the tides of madness
drown these flames?

will the sense of time stretch
interminably until sleep?

will a lifetime of unabashed tenderness
be displayed on your face?

will the profound sadness of our losses
be folded into the wholeness of life?

will our struggle
bring forth
the endless parting,
the sinking eyelid,
the final collapse?

and will i be remembered at all
by these thoughts and words
i leave behind?

the architecture of memory

reading dostovesky's
notes from the underground,
on an airplane
30,000 feet in the clouds.

i'm thinking
of kneeling at the side of my bed
as blood pumps through my bruised spirit.

i'm thinking
of life,
and how people waste so much time,
and i know this because
of the eloquent gestures
of opening and closing flowers.

i'm thinking of summer,
and how it seemed so much longer last year.

and i'm thinking
that i will do my best
to never allow myself
to be defeated by this world.

and i will accept
the architecture of memory
and remembering
and dreaming.

and remembering again
and dreaming again.

words from grandmother to grandson
(for greta loftus silich: 1911-2000)

last night my grandmother called and said:
"from reading your words,
i can see how what's in your heart
and what's in your head
can lend great confusion to a career in law.
i can see how you can be in constant turmoil.

"your grandfather didn't like lawyers
and always maintained that there
wasn't one honest lawyer in the world.

"you know, you don't have to spend your life
getting even with people or
trying to blame someone for life's accidents or
trying to punish someone for being human or
trying to accumulate as much money as possible."

after we hung up, i noticed a letter
she had written me a few days ago
sitting on the desk. it began:

"my wishes for you are three:
1 - patience enough to toil until
some good is accomplished
2 - strength enough to battle the
difficulties and overcome them
3 - hope enough to remove the anxious
fears concerning the future."

the letter continued,

"through your heritage and some unknown
power, you have strength, wisdom, and
determination. may you always believe in the
special abilities that have been created for you.

feel assured, whatever your future, great
loves accompany you whichever way you go."

i taped the letter to the refrigerator,
turned the ringer off,
sat down on the bed,
and wiped the tears from my eyes.

obscene

our
eyelids
will
close
and
life's
poverty
will
continue
to
shout
obscenities
at
the
rest
of
the
world,

and
it
will
remain
the
unending
tragedy
of
our
existence.

splendid

life
is
sometimes
more
splendid
than
the
hand
waving
goodbye

because
stone crumbles,
marble cracks,
wood rots,
and people leave,

but fragile
good thoughts
remain,

and these words
are only an echo
of your words.

exit laughing

when your time comes,
and if you're lucky enough
to be conscious of the moment,
remember that behind it all
there is always a hint of desperation,
which is ok,
because returning to sleep
is the achievement,
rising in the morning,
the victory.

we are all going to die,
which should be enough
for kindness to win out,
but it isn't, and that is heartbreaking.

more importantly,
remember when you're ready to go,
you'll do so
just beneath
the dreams of poets,
and you'll
exit laughing,
singing your songs
in your own way,
because art alone
gently endures.

2 cheeseburgers

i remember
the night
when i was in
miami beach
with her
and we were violently robbed at gunpoint.

during a high speed chase
of over 100 mph,
we were shot at 16 times,
with 11 bullets hitting our rented car,
but we somehow made it through
and survived
without so much as a scratch.

after spending
most of the night
with the local police,
answering questions
and looking through
volumes of mugshots,
we returned to our hotel
with no money,
no watches,
no keys,
no camera,
no credit cards,
no identification,
and a car with a windshield
covered with bullet holes.

we told the hotel manager
what happened.
he looked down,
shuffled his feet,
and said,

"i'm really sorry
about your experience."

he paused, then continued,

"i have a great idea.
why don't you guys
order some food,
sit out on the front steps,
and watch the sun rise
over the ocean?
it'll be up soon."

we looked at each other,
smiled for the first time that night,
ordered
2 cheeseburgers,
2 large fries,
2 large cokes,
and headed out to the front
of the hotel.

the sun began
to do its thing,
and the food arrived
in perfect time.

and so there we were,
at 5:30 in the morning,
enjoying some of the best cheeseburgers
we had ever sunk our teeth into.

she put her hand
softly on the back
of my neck
and smiled that smile
that kept me returning to her.

there really was
nothing else to do
except sit back
and listen to the ocean
while trying
not to think
about anything else
other than the fact
that this really was
a good place to be,
as good a place as any,
when you're trying to
endure this life
and the quiet labor of existence.

most evenings

most
evenings
you
will
find
me
at home,

writing
and
waiting
for
her

like
the
last
flower
of
summer.

what i'll always have

i've
enjoyed
their beds
and their wine,
the private communions,
and the astounding intimacies
of our brief stories.

i listened
the best i could,
and everything seemed
to arrive
at the right moment.

when i look back on my time
in those apartments,
i'll always have
us reading neruda,
resting on bare arms,
sitting on fire escapes,
and sharing pure laughter.

and there will always be
the dream of
watching
the hands of time
circle gently,
postponing
the
kiss
goodbye.

9 blocks

picked up my 2 daughters
from school today,
and my 5-year-old said
her sneakers were bothering her
and she couldn't walk.

my 3-year-old conveniently
said the same thing.
both started crying.
i said ok,
daddy will carry you home.

so i picked them up,
one in each arm, and
they put their heads on my shoulders,
and off we went.
me in my suit for work,
including dress shoes.

i said to myself, with each step:
i'm sorry this world won't keep you safe,
but i'll try for 9 blocks.

the pain and numbness in my arms,
and the ache in my feet and hips,
were a small price to pay for the attempt.

i continued, to myself again:

your first home was your mother's belly,
your second home will be your father's arms.

i will carry you for as long as you let me.
i will carry you when your little legs are tired.
i will carry you when you don't feel well.
i will carry you just to keep you close to me.

i will carry you for no reason at all.

and i will carry you still,
when my body gives out
and my heart stops beating.

threat

everything threatens us,
but nothing as much as time.

and at long last,
i am tired,
but my lungs still fill
and my bones no longer feel hollow.

the unknown remains unknown,
the unexplainable remains unexplained,
and some things
just can't be put into words.

like the little boy
who starts each morning
by praying to himself not to cry today
or the old man
who wakes up at 3 o'clock in the morning
every day and asks,
"where is she?"

radiant child
(for mia, age 3)

the grace of this love covers us
if we look close enough.

and you,
my little radiant child,
it is for you
that i write every sentence,
ask every question,
and hold every belief.

you, with unerring attention
to everything around you,
are at once
reflective and elusive

and a pure, noble gift
to humanity.

man with a book

there's a guy who sleeps in front
of my apartment building
in a cardboard box.

during the day,
he stands on top of the subway grates
for heat.

he walks up to cars
stopped at the light,
taps the sides and back,
and then returns to the
sidewalk.

he'll also stick out his arm and
let it brush against someone walking by.

maybe he does this to see
if they're alive or to see if he is.

the other day,
he sat on the corner of 63rd and madison
reading a copy of proust's
in search of lost time.

i walked by
and he yelled:
"you're no different than me!"

i looked at the faded book cover
shining under the blue sky
and his eyes just as bright,

and he was right;
he certainly is no different
than the rest of us.

perhaps at
moments like this,
he's a little more splendid
than the rest of the bums
with their white shirts
and colorful ties
heading off to their
nine to fives.

dear mr. hemingway

ernest,

you are
as beautiful as the bulls in pamplona,
as beautiful as the brave sun in key west,
as beautiful as the green hills in africa,
as beautiful as the women in paris,
as beautiful as life.

thank you for your help.

best regards,

stephan

under the palm leaves

just last week
i was in florida
lying under the palm leaves,
feeling the sun on my arms,
and easing back a glass of wine.

i watched my brother
resting on one of the lounges,
listening to music,
and my eyes filled triumphantly
because he makes the world
a better place.

i finished my drink
and all i could think
was that the gods
have been good to us.

rejection

remember
they will
try to break you,
like they often do,
hour after hour.

but they fail to realize
that rejection
and criticism
and envy are the achievements.

it forces you
to scream
without raising your voice,
and to show the world who you are
by taking exactly what they criticize
and nurturing it,
making it yours alone.

that's where the magic lies.

that's what sets you apart.

so continue doing exactly
what you're doing
in writing and in life

and these moments
will turn into words,

these words
into pages,

and these pages
into books.

your face

i walk alone
staring at the
faded storefronts
and solitary lampposts,
fully aware that it's
the unseen wounds
and the elegance of scars
that hold the meaning.

i walk
to the west side
and watch
slabs of ice
shuffle their way
down the hudson,
as only echoes remain
where there once was love.

i am unable
to grasp the meaning
in all this,
until i close my eyes
and see your face…

and you are
more poetic
than the
35,000 volumes of poetry
in the new york public library.

the unknown great

in all periods of history, there are
those who find themselves apart from
the rest, and humanity is very much
indebted to those same people.

it is not the known great, but the great
    who die unknown,
that make the difference.

success

i think of the generations before me

and how van gogh couldn't sell a single painting
until he killed himself.

how dekooning faded with alzheimers.

how modigliani died from meningitis.

how dylan thomas drank until his heart gave out.

and how rimbaud wrote *a season in hell* when he was 19
and then gave up writing for the rest of his life.

i sit up wondering
if i'll ever get these words down
the way i want to,
and then i remember reading a story about
pablo neruda and how he wrote with green ink
because green is the color of hope.

and i return to these words
more wondrous than ever,
and the rest of the night will be so too.

me & that famous artist
(feb. 25, 1998)

at the museum of modern art

dinner for a group of artists
and collectors and art dealers.

at my table,
a very well-known artist sat quietly.

in between his gentle smiles,
he filled his time with
glasses of red wine.

after his 3rd
he turned to me
and whispered:

"how did i get here?
i must have made
a wrong turn
and ended up here."

i smiled
and he continued:

"i really hate
this stuff,
don't you?"

"yeah, it's pretty bad,"
i answered.
"i'm just here so i can pay the rent."

"i understand," he said.

i asked if he would like
more red wine.

"yes, please,"
he answered, moving his glass closer
to the edge of the table,

"and keep it coming."

i filled his glass,
he smiled,
and i did the same.

paris has difficulty breathing

without solitude,
life would be a mistake.

so i try to stay still
and think of a faraway summer
where the divine sun arrives for us,

and where
your beauty is such
that even paris has difficulty breathing.

almost

there are a dozen ways to drive a man crazy.
there are a dozen ways to destroy a man's heart.

i have spent my whole life fighting
for the hours to do what i want.

in a world of 7.6 billion people,
i have almost succeeded,
with a little help
from the unanticipated grace of strangers,
the disarmingly simple pleasures of an ordinary day,
and the flashes of memory
that always keep you by my side.

burning

i think of you
and your face reminds me
of what a face looks like
after a long cry,
bursting forth with hope
burning the day.

unwrap all your wounds,
let the mournful lamentations
remain undiminished,

and rescue me
from the calamitous
tale of humanity.

unclasp

i watched you
unclasp the back of your bathing suit
as you prepared for a day of rest.

i found such harmony
in this beauty,

beauty not found in magazines or movies,

that took me
from stardust
to longing,

reminding me
that the immense weight of time
and the memory
of those first nights together
are all that will remain.

i will carry these with me
wherever i go,
and they will allow my soul
to be
reconsidered,
reformatted,
and revived.

tributes

allow the mistakes you make
to be the tributes of your life.

a hand in the sunsets

i believe
your beauty
will continue
to spread itself out
over the centuries.

i believe
you will always remain
in the shimmer
of those candles
in that corner café.

i believe you
give the sea its silence.

and i believe you have
a hand in the sunsets.

for dad, after your latest brain scan
(may 2018)

we are your symphony,
you are the music.

we are your novel,
you are the literature.

we are your film,
you are the cinema.

we are your paintings,
you are the museum.

we salute you.

we console your grandchildren.

we ask for the great
and the good of this world
to arrive for you today.

we drink in
these faultless days,
which we will not soon forget.

when the sadness comes,
it will not be limited
to those in this room,
so take it all in.

time is running out
for all of us,
but these chronicles of life,
unhurriedly receding and rising,
will provide us with
our greatest intimacy.

we love you.

writing

i've loaded
and unloaded trucks,
dug ditches,
mowed lawns,
served food,
poured drinks,
stocked shelves,
planted trees,
laid bricks,
poured cement,
trimmed hedges,
mopped floors,
and even put on the suit
and tightened the necktie.

the rest of the time
is spent writing.

public approval
and popularity
will always remain
the divine lie,
the deferred dream,
the great decline,
the withering resistance,
the graceless effort,
the undignified profane,
but never
the final death blow.

which reminds me of
an american painter's
warmly written obituary.

it said:

"he avoided publicity
throughout his life,
ignored his critics
and seemed to welcome the privacy
that came with unpopularity."

the apartment walls

i breathe in the air
of these new york streets
from my open screened window.

on nights like these,
the apartment walls
hold the answers,
and they sometimes
push in
from all sides,

trying to crush
the
ancient
words
of
lovers
and
the
departed
landmarks
of
youth.

most nights

most nights
i feel
at peace,
without any disquiet,
but tonight
i would have liked
to talk to you.

i would have told you that
i once slept overnight
on a park bench
in pamplona
and there was a certain
stillness about it that
has never been repeated.

i would have told you that
you are exemplary for your
listening and understanding
and for your sacrifice of tomorrow.

i would have told you that
time will discover you,
so you have to fight for every minute.

i would have told you that
what is most ordinary,
most basic, and most familiar,
is also what is most eloquent.

and i would have told you that
these are my sweetest words for you,
but also the saddest,
and there's a certain stillness
about that too.

getting to heaven without dying

when it was over,
she placed my head
on her chest,
and i listened to the
thumping of her heart
as she glided her fingers
around the back of my hair.

and there i was,
all of 30 years old,
realizing you
don't necessarily have to die
in order to get to heaven.

a day

sometimes it comes down to
watching the brave sun in august.

and sometimes
it's just remembering
that one room
when you were alone
and glad to be alone.

arias

i've never passed a man on the street
whom i admired.

most beautiful women never smile.

most criminals are not behind bars.

rust crawls into the souls of most,
and we've all been given minds and bodies
and names that won't last.

but right now i'm too tired to be lonely,
and life feels a little
like the unread poet
bending down to pick up his broken button.

but words matter.

and the words written in the past matter.

they're with us,
patiently waiting for new words,
reverentially striving
to achieve something
by which we might be remembered.

much the same way
places speak to you more eloquently
when you are just about to leave them.

victory

this is the victory:
the smashed face never giving in.

anything that brings you closer to love
(for mia)

i sat on the edge of the twin bed
with my 3-year-old, mia.

she tossed and turned
until she found her spot of comfort
for the night.

she put her little arm around me
and mixed her tiny fingers with mine,
and with a small hint of a smile,
she fell fast asleep.

the sense of time
stretched interminably
until the very moment
when the emotional weight
and our now enduring legacy
tired the sun
and folded him away for the night.

how do you make it?

bukowski had to reach 51
before he could pay the rent
with his writing.

titian had assistants
tie paintbrushes to his hands when his
arthritis became too much.

dostoevsky did 4 years of hard labor
in siberia for printing articles
against the government.

miller worked for western union
for 12 years to pay his bills.

and whitman had to hire a brooklyn print shop
to publish his 1st edition of *leaves of grass*.

so i'll leave you now
with this little piece of a poem,

and i'll continue to write these words,

which sometimes have the ability
to break my back,
today and tomorrow
and today again,

while the age of man flutters
beneath the howls of outrage.

an old lady and a dog

i walked over to lexington avenue,
where i had parked my car,
and saw an old lady
standing on the corner.

she was crying and she turned to me
and said,

"please help me, please."

i noticed her dog
lying by her side, motionless.

she told me the dog collapsed in the heat
and that no cabs would pick them up.

i lifted the dog in my arms
and carried him 2 blocks to my car.

i wrapped him in a blanket
and drove them to
an animal hospital on 65th & 2nd.

as i was leaving,
she said,

"you're an angel.
 you're my angel!
 do you believe in angels?"

i looked at her sad eyes
and the eyes of her dying dog
and said,

"i'm not sure,
 but i guess it's about time
 some of them came out of hiding."

she laughed a great, deep laugh
and i wished her luck.

she gently kissed my cheek
and said thank you.

i headed toward 3rd avenue,

and saw my girlfriend
standing across the street.
she looked more exquisite
than ever
and was waiting just for me.

for you only

let me walk past you
and get that feeling for a brief moment.

let my soul fill with unspecific tragedy
because life
hides from so many of us,
and not everyone desires
a safe and scripted version.

give me this,
and we can postpone
our bids of farewell
to a world that has forgotten dignity.

give me this,
and i will fight the brutality
against the kindhearted way of life,

give me this,
and i will continue
to tell stories about lost love,
and roads not taken,
and what matters most,

which is my daughters sleeping
with their arms around each other,
with an unbridled sweetness
that is completely indescribable.

bleed the sky

i gave them
a casual goodbye
and headed for the door.

they thought
i was just going
for the night,
but i had made my escape.

and they will not find me
unless they search
beneath the smile
hiding the sorrows
that belong to us all.

and the rest of the days
will be mine.

and i'll embrace
the unseen
risks and rewards
of being human.

somewhere

it was an afternoon
full of shade,
and in that shade
we rested,
as men often do
when offered
refuge from war.

we just sat there
with our thoughts.

and it was then
i realized

poems still need to be written,

songs still need to be sung,

and paintings still need to be painted,

because somewhere
young boys are waiting
for their first kiss,

and somewhere
someone is turning out the light
and waiting breathlessly for tomorrow.

the ones

be careful
because the ones
who bag the groceries,
open the doors,
hammer the nails,
sweep the floors,
and open bottles of wine,
may just be the ones
who have
the finest hands to
ever curl around pencils
and paintbrushes
and piano keys.

nothing

i fall in love with
beautiful strangers
ten times a day.

it's magical.

it's all i have.

i have nothing.

ars artia gratis

i sit here tonight
with these thoughts
accompanied by
cezzane in provence
gauguin in tahiti
da vinci in florence
rodin in paris
giacometti in geneva
rembrandt in amsterdam
warhol in montauk
caravaggio in naples
basquiat in new york
goya in bordeaux
velasquez in madrid
twombly in rome
matisse in morocco,
van gogh in arles,
and pollock in east hampton.

i thank you
for the soulful shimmering
under the surface of your canvases,
the cups of salvation,
and the bread of life.

these are my prayers for you all.

indifferent gods

it's the truth
that i understand.

it's the reason
i can look at the face
of the factory worker
and know that he has more soul
than 1,000 of your
favorite poets combined.

and it is why
i sit here in silence
one minute
and then
shake my fist
in the face of
unfailingly
indifferent gods
the next.

easy day

he waited
in the blue seats
of the airport,
glancing at the five or six people
waiting alongside him,
and hoped that none of them
would be sitting next to him
on the flight back to new york.

the waiting itself
didn't bother him;
after all,
this was as good a place
as any to sit and wait.

the sun outside
was stronger than ever
even though it was
late december,
and the year was finally
coming to an end.

he stared at the seams
coming apart along the side of his pants,
which made him think about the
house not paid for
and the job that could end
on a moment's notice.

but this
would still be an easy day
because he would soon see her,
and all the pain would slip away
when the sleep of her body
and her dark eyes
closed for the night,
next to him
and only him.

not alone

i write these quiet words
hoping they will help someone
who wakes in the middle of the night
know that they are not alone.

across the sand

in the sweetness
of this drowsy summer afternoon,
i watch a girl
in a brown bikini
walk across the sand
and it makes everything seem okay.

left and right she moves
as her spirit
mixes with the ocean wind
and the bending palms.

but here is where you must be careful,
because this summer day
can also break you into a million pieces
and defeat all that remains
in your american soul.

the beat that skips my heart

it was a day after heavy rain
and i waited for you
and for what i hoped
would be our first words.

i introduced myself
and asked for a moment of your time.
you smiled, said ok, and mentioned
that you were walking home.

i walked with you and told you
that i loved the way
you curl your hair behind your ear
and how you gently put your hand
over your mouth when you yawn.

in you,
i found a world's worth of tenderness.

in you,
i found a well-timed gift.

and in you,
i simply found the beat that skips my heart.

how to do this right?

live an ordinary life
with extraordinary love.

how to do this bravely?

let the blood of poets
flow over
the bones of christ.

a fine morning

you're always the one
i want to talk to
before i go to sleep,
and i can't wait
to sleep beside you
because you sleep
more peacefully
than anyone
i've ever known.

and when
the music
plays low,
we will set ablaze
these long days
of evening calm
and slowly
turn this
blue night
into morning.

time

i won't stop until the moment
my heart gives out.

this is more about life than death.

every word written is a last word,
an obituary,
a testament to something left behind,
something contributed.

these verses will
endure through the centuries.

these minutes of life will
address your particular sorrows.

the subtlety of your soul will
defeat the inhumanity
of not having enough time.

and if not,
will you please rescue me
from this boundary of oblivion?

conversation with emma
(april 14, 2018)

"daddy,
i feel sad today.
i think i did something wrong.

"i was at the park and saw a boy who had bad marks all
over his face, and no one was playing with him.

"he looked like that boy in the movie nana showed me."

"the movie *wonder*, emma?"

"yeah, daddy, that's the one. the book too."

"ok, tell me what happened."

"i was looking at him
and i wanted to go over and say:
'are you okay? how are you feeling?'"

emma started crying and said:

"but i didn't, daddy.
i was too shy.
i should have said something. i think he felt bad."

"it's ok, emma, you thought about it, and that's enough.
please don't cry. you are a sweet girl and very kind."

"i want to be kind, daddy.
i should have talked to him."

"it's ok,
you are kind.
you are our wonder."

and you are simply the reason
every tear makes it way down my cheek
the very moment the sun dips under the horizon.

infinite worlds of nature

your entrance was followed fairly quickly by your exit,
and the whole grand pattern of human endeavor,
once bounded by time,
is now just an outline of life.

a life
in which the violently unexpected breaking of vows
arrived on that early may 1st morning,
just a few hours after my birthday.

our reality and our shadow
deserved much better than this.

i will live this life with more care now
and be comforted by davinci's
infinite worlds of nature,
which reminds us that there are 422 living trees
for every human being on earth.

that makes me feel good.

and although it might seem as if life doesn't balance out all
the bad at once,
it's supposed to across our lifetime.

and if it doesn't, then
search to restore the tenderness lost,
contribute something to the immeasurable passing of time,
make beauty possible somewhere,
rejoice in the bonds you form,
the choices you make,
and the paths you choose.

race ahead of history to wilder shores,
read deeply,

listen carefully,
watch closely.

the rawness of these moments remain.
the celebrations of history remain.
the fragments of a lifetime remain.
the pleasures of ruins remain.

and as long as i have a breath,

i will breathe everything into my two little girls,
because these feelings haven't faded yet
from this old fragile heart,

and they never will.

tired

"you're tired,"
i told myself.

and when i'm tired,
i always think of you.

half

half-remembered
half-imagined
half-haunting my days...

these unfinished,
fragmentary recollections
will remain.

and the end,
although always unexpected,
will bring
rest, recovery, and reflection.

beauty is always
where you don't expect it.

remember your sense of place.
remember certain people,
certain buildings,
certain feelings,
certain memories,
all shaped
by rediscovered stories,
long gone.

and the remainder?

hold it.

hold the unseen possibility
and let it bring you back
into the world,
ever so slowly.

sadness

perhaps
sadness
is life's way
of reminding us
that we haven't
been forgotten
after all.

echoes

only the memories remain,

and our memories
will become echoes
where there once was love.

artists

with all the distractions
of work and life,
i'm still able to spend
a good deal of my time
just walking and thinking.

all my heroes are still artists,
and they are always with me,
searing beneath
the surface of a once young soul.

it's why i'm able to sit here
in the artist's studio i built
for my two daughters,
with its cedar shingles, barn doors,
windows, table, chairs, and easels,
where we spend weekends
painting blank canvases, and paper,
and old photographs, and shells from the beach,
even the floors and walls.

it is where we treat ourselves
to the much-needed moments of presence,
making peace with
whatever time we have left.

hoping they learn
to be personal with what they create
and care about the moon and the planets
and the days and the seasons.

there is not much else i can do
except keep inviting these moments in,
which continually heal my heart
that beats more slowly with time.

loving properly

i wrote a poem once
about how i felt
that, after all these centuries,
we still haven't learned to love properly.

but now i'm thinking
maybe we're born knowing how to love,
and we just lose our way
for long stretches of time.

outrun the disadvantages

you still give me
something
resembling truth
as i outrun
the disadvantages
of staying kind.

and there are many things:
sacred obligations,
faithful protections,
loyal engagements,
elegant conversations,
contented hours,
and the unspoken privacies
that should keep us together.

and there's the
advice not given,
promises unmet,
envelopes not stamped,
songs unsung,
stories not recorded,
photographs not taken,
exhausted words,
and 1,000 memories forgotten.

it's our tenuous hold
on earth,
fighting against
the age of the universe.

so don't take the money.
do you hear me?
do not take the money.

have a quiet dinner,
go see a movie,
define your times
and the times of your children.

give them nourishment

and liberty
and endurance.

give them love,
but not your beliefs.

let them run free,
let them go;
they were never yours to begin with.

give them
understated
unpretentious
unbridled
dreams.

always
expect to die young
so your borrowed time
is where you invest
all the love you have to give.

art will bring exaltation;
let it enfold you:

the great words
the great images
the great music.

let them wash over you.

let the richness
of human nature

push the boundaries
of all possibility.

these are the instruments
of a measured life.

do not lose the
indescribable pureness
in yourself.

do not erase their memory of you.

do not avoid the struggle;
it's the solution to
the question of who you are.

do not avoid physical labor:

carve the wood,
make the fire,
carry the bags,
pump the gas,
pick the flowers,
sweep the floor,
and walk
wherever and whenever you can.

disregard the outcomes.

wrap your arms around these
worthy challenges and
meaningful inconveniences.

be at ease with your unease.

find the haunting, undeniable,
and beautifully unfinished thoughts
among your fractured memory.

remember the moments that seem
ordinary at the time:
accidental encounters,
like a chance meeting
on a park bench
or at a coffee shop,
will likely prove
the most unforgettable.

these are my thoughts.
these are my hymns of reliance.

these are my songs of truthfulness
becoming the inexplicable glow of hope.

it is why i'm able to sit here
weeping while my children
sleep soundly in the next room.

and in this silence,
we become sadder,
older, wiser.

but the elegance of time
guides me into this old age
with extraordinary generosity
and refinement.

and your sweetness
provides me with
the profound dignity of humanity.

tonight will be
the longest night of them all

in memory of all the libraries and bookstores
filled with old stories and pages,
dusty with age, forgiven by time...

it's important to have the beating heart of an artist,

to keep your work deliberately unfinished,

to have the ability to trust uncertain things,

to stay aware of your sense of timelessness,

to let absolute aloneness unfold upon you,

to take in the sun's slow passage
and its answering shadows,

and to float above it all.

this will be your enduring contribution
because
tonight
will
be
the
longest
night
of
them
all.

postscript

some early words that helped…

letter #1
(january 28, 1994)

Dear Stephan,

It's late. And the reason I am still up is because I started reading your book of poems and couldn't stop.

Stephan, I am simply blown away. Truly.

Poems and lyrics to songs have always been important to me. When my mind is cluttered or my heart is sad, these words on paper have always been here for me–straightened out my confusion or despair.

It's funny, but advice from wise people is always so good to get, but unfortunately the exact words aren't always with you.

This incredible, priceless book of yours will always be.

Love,

P.B.

letter #2
(february 23, 1994)

Dear Stephan,

Just a little note to thank you for allowing me to read your poetry. It seems to be such a personal journey, changing and maturing.

To translate your emotions and conceptualize your thoughts into verse is an art. To me, a poet bares his soul and in doing so shares the innocence and the complexities that form the collage that is his life.

He can only hope that in this vulnerable state he is understood and can touch that common chord that ties us all together.

Your poetry touched me, Stephan.

I hope one day to read more.

Fondest regards,

J.M.

letter #3
(september, 1997)

My Dearest Stephan -

To you I am writing on this quiet, lonely night in Harlem's outskirts. It is your voice I long to hear and your many contradictions that I long to cherish. I want you to know that your voice as a poet and a person is strong and is something to be wholly believed in. You see the world through invaluable eyes–eyes which experience the pain and beauty of this oh so complicated world–eyes which perceive and attempt to deny the many facets of existence that constitute humanity, that embody all that it is to live.

Stephan, I love you as a person - as an artist - as you–someone struggling so sincerely with the world, in a soul that cries out for truth. I hope many, many things for you - one of which is the ability to trust yourself - in your inner strength and courage - not what you "should" be, but who you are. You have much to offer the world. Internalize what you always told me: that "art alone gently endures" and that you, my dear friend who feels so much, are an artist.

Love,

J.F.

letter #4
(august 23, 2001)

Dear Stephan,

The resolve to write this letter is in no sense trivial, given the circumstances. I intend it to supplant a dialogue we never had. This resolve came as a result of a deliberation that I must not permit my good manners to slip, even with excuses.

After all, I have let many months elapse without ever finding an opportunity to tell you in person how much I enjoyed your poetry, and how meaningful it was to discover a kindred spirit in the verses and collections that persuaded and pardoned my indulgence.

I was struck by the maturity of your feelings and the simplicity of your eloquence. The idealistic stubbornness cheered my heart with the spirit of camaraderie.

Your profound yearnings of the heart and scars of love elicited a pathos so comparable to me. Will the light of publication ever shine upon these volumes of verse speaking largely of affairs of human hearts? Hope has a saving grace, you so encouraged in one of the poems.

To read is to live life vicariously, but to write is the real thing. The latter demands a much daring passion and requires sacrifice and devotion. I admire your spirit of perseverance and your efforts to indulge always your poetic voice.

You have chosen a path inconvenient to financial rewards, and clearly incongruous with the communal urge to chase material merrymaking. A poet rarely fails to nourish a suffering soul at the expense of his own agony.

You have certainly inspired me, not that you so intended to lift me so very high. I thought I soared far, when a decade ago, unable to resist the lure of distant horizons, I lifted my languishing self from China. I am now shown there are more heights to aspire to.

The rugged path you chose has deposited you to a lonely climb. I pray that the blessings of bonne chance will be bestowed along your literary way, and you are kept company by those few who share your convictions and endure your perseverance.

You have an audience and a rooter in me.

(Having been able to rid my chest of this burden of words at long last, I already feel better about life in general.)

Yours always,

R.W.

words from my brother
(may 10, 1996)

Stephan -

A few words to collect my thoughts - mostly thoughts of you. What a strange year for us both . . . love and loss, joy and pain dealt us both evenly. Yet I feel no real pain in the face of my one truth in life: my brother, myself.

We share the same cells from the bottom to the top and a bond of love and fate that our life's loves, whoever they may be, will never so much as make a mark.

I always envision my death scene with a flurry of memories of both of us . . .

You are the rock I will break myself upon: solid, unwavering.

Ironic that you are so solid yet you have cared so little for the things that society values as marks of solidity.

Anyway . . . just a few words after 27 years, I've never been kind to words as you are, but sometimes we scratch down these marks only to give a clue (never to really express . . . impossible as you know), a clue to the infinite realm of love we all have, we all possess, and the infinite realm of love we will always live with.

I love you, Stephan . . . always did, always will.

- Robert

a father's thoughts

When I'm not with them, I wish I were. I have a soulful need to guide and protect them, yet I want them to grow and be men on their own.

When I'm with them, I don't want to interfere with their dreams, hopes, desires, yet I want to be a part of all that.

I suffer because I love them so much. I find it hard to let go, to let them fall and fail. I want to support and uplift, but I've got to release myself from them. And this forced and necessary separation is so necessary for them, so painful for me. They are successes by all who know them, by all who meet them.

If i die tonight, my life and fatherhood have been a success because of them.

I love and honor my wife, their mother. There is so much of her in them. She has as much pain as I do regarding their growth and subsequent separation from us. She's so wonderful. I am so fortunate.

Can I ever let them know how much they mean to me? That they are the reason I continue to work and slave at my profession—not for my ego or any glory, but so i can give them things I had not—make their lives easier and not so painful.

God, I love them so. And I feel so deeply for that union. I wish they never grew up. It's so bittersweet, yet so necessary.

these 'thoughts' were written by my father in the back cover of an old book of fiction he was reading. my brother robert borrowed the book and came across this by accident sometime in august 1996.

acknowledgements

I want to thank my publisher Marina Aris and the Brooklyn Writers Press, as well as my editor, Judi Heidel, for their intelligence and diligence, and their belief and guidance.

I also want to thank the following for their inspiration and pure beauty:

The grandfathers I never met

The grandmothers I loved and lost

The sound of my mother's slippers across the kitchen floor

The smell of my father's shirts

The gentleness and generosity of my brother

My parents' life-long friends

My childhood

Walking my daughters to school every morning

Sarah Wright's warmth, gift giving and educating at the little flower shop on 80th and 3rd

Familiar strangers

Jennifer Fontao's ephemeral uniqueness, intelligence, beauty and instagram account

Louise Fontao's smile and home cooked meals

Arthur Klein and Susan Taylor's unwavering support and endless hospitality

Art teachers

Music teachers

Poetry teachers

History teachers

Literature teachers

Carpenters

Plumbers

Electricians

Police officers

Landscapers

Painters

Dog walkers

Watchmakers

Booksellers

Factory workers

Toy makers
Bartenders

Marlon Brando
Martin Luther King
The Dalai Lama
Buddha
Christopher Hitchens
John Richardson
Robert Hughes
Winston Churchill
Alexander McQueen
Brunello Cucinelli
Azzedine Alaia
Alber Elbaz
Roman and Williams
Pat Tillman
Eustace Conway
Anthony Bourdain
And all the people who can cook a good meal

SOME PLACES
55 Austin Place
22 Valencia Avenue
1104 Grand Cay Drive
1045 Papermill Court
1 West 72nd Street
26 East 63rd Street
40 East 65th Street
475 Springs Fireplace Road
155 East 76th Street
Soho at night
Prince Street
Mercer Street
Greene Street
Little West 12th Street
Grove Street
Park Avenue

Madison Avenue
The city of Rome
The city of Florence
The city of Paris
The city of London
The city of Mumbai
East Hampton
Palm Beach
Big Sur
The Carlyle Hotel
The Belmond San Michelle
The Line

SOME WRITERS
Henry Miller
Anais Nin
Charles Bukowski
Albert Camus
Leonard Cohen
Patti Smith
Ernest Hemingway
Jack Kerouac
Joan Didion
Rudyard Kipling
Walt Whitman
John-Paul Sarte
John Steinbeck
Mary Oliver
Pablo Neruda
John Fante
Hunter Thompson
Rainer Marie Rilke
Haruki Murakami
Gabriel Garcia Marquez
Max Ehrmann
Henry David Thoreau
Ursula Le Guin
Edna St. Vincent Millay

Fyodor Dostoyevsky
Oscar Wilde
Alain de Botton
Stephen Hawking
Dorothy Parker
William Blake
Robinson Jeffers
Marcus Aurelius
Pico Iyer
Oliver Sacks
Kahlil Gibran
Sylvia Path
Allen Ginsberg
Toni Morrison
Harold Norse
Gregory Corso
EE Cummings
Friedrich Nietzsche
WH Auden
James Baldwin
Antoine de Saint-Exupéry
Jim Harrison
Jiddu Krishnamurti
Charles Buadelaire
Federico Garcia Lorca
Gertrude Stein
Langston Hughes
William Butler Yeats
John Keats

SOME ARTISTS
Jean Michel Basquiat
Amedeo Modigliani
Frida Kahlo
Mark Rothko
Cy Twombly
Georgia O'Keefe
Francesco Clemente

Alberto Giacometti
Agnes Martin
Rene Ricard
Tracey Emin
Henri Matisse
Leonardo DaVinci
Michelangelo Caravaggio
Michelangelo Buonarroti
Vincent Van Gogh
Francis Bacon
Cecily Brown
Paul Cezzane
Andy Warhol
Julian Schnabel's plate paintings
Jackson Pollock
Pablo Picasso's blue and rose periods
Banksy
Graffiti artists and Street artists

SOME PHOTOGRAPHERS
Robert Doisneau
Henri Cartier-Bresson
Jeanloup Sieff
Peter Beard
Dorothea Lange
Edward Weston
Ellen Von Unworth
Peter Lindbergh
Helmut Newton
Brassai
JR

SOME MUSICIANS
The Bedrocks
Thom Yorke (Radiohead)
Robert Smith (The Cure)
Bob Marley
Keith Richards

David Bowie
Joe Strummer (The Clash)
Nina Simone
John Lennon
Stewart Copeland
Freddy Mercury
Sade
Morrissey (The Smiths)
Dave Gahan (Depeche Mode)
Miles Davis
Deborah Harry
Johnny Rotten (The Sex Pistols)
Nick Cave
Nick Drake
Iggy Pop
Ian Curtis (Joy Division)
Jeff Buckley
Billie Holiday

SOME BOOKS
The Old Man and the Sea
The Diving Bell and the Butterfly
Burning in Water, Drowning in Flame
The Grapes of Wrath
Love in the Time of Cholera
The Catcher in the Rye
Great Expectations
Leaves of Grass
On the Road
The Waste Land
You Get So Alone At Times that It Just Makes Sense
The Flowers of Evil
The Rum Diary
The Count of Monte Cristo
A Season in Hell
Women in Love
Of Mice and Men
The Wisdom of the Heart

Stand Still Like the Hummingbird
The Last Night of the Earth Poems
The Air Conditioned Nightmare
The Year of Magical Thinking
Meditations
Run with the Hunted
Whitman's Wild Children

SOME CHILDREN'S BOOKS
The Little Prince
The Giving Tree
The Story of Bertolt
Cry, Heart, But Never Break
Layla's Happiness
A Velocity of Being

SOME MOVIES
Il Postino
The Intouchables
Cinema Paradiso
Breathless
The Big Blue
Amelie
Last Night
A Good Year
The Family Man
Basquiat
Before Night Falls
Barfly
Love Actually
Trainspotting
Pope of Greenwich Village
Wings of Desire
Blade Runner

SOME FLOWERS
Hydrangeas
Peonies

Orchids
Dandelions
Daisies
Tulips
Lilacs
Hyacinths
Jasmine
Lavender
Gardenias
Lilies
Magnolias
Sunflowers
Wisteria

SOME THINGS
Thanksgiving
Christmas
Biographies
Obituaries
Headstones
Quotes
Non-fiction
Documentaries
The philosophy of wabi-sabi
Window seats on airplanes
The monuments of Washington DC at night
Rows of limestone townhouses
Cast-iron downtown lofts
Outdoor cafes
Storefront windows
Street vendors
City rooftops
Cobblestone streets
Courtyards
Playgrounds
Public libraries
Community gardens
Movie soundtracks

First editions
Quiet restaurants
Bicycles
Surfboards
Vespas
Triumph Motorcycles
Norton Motorcycles
Indian Motorcycles
Rizzoli bookstores
Assouline bookstores
All bookstores
Wood burning fireplaces
Outdoor fire pits
Bamboo
White Oak Trees
White Birch Trees
Cedar Trees
Pine Trees
The quiet calm after weeping
The feel of my bare feet in the sand
The laziness of Sunday
The simple pleasures of an ordinary day
Unhurried walks
Moments stirred by laughter
Pieces of forgotten music
True sensations of kindness
Eyes full of trust
Us sleeping in the afternoon sun
The slow beat of your heart on top of mine
The exquisiteness of your face in the morning
The quietness after
The open road
The unadorned truth
The smell of the breeze rising from the ocean
The layers of sunlight through bedroom windows
The sound of a few notes of music
The naked back on the other side of the bed
The clouds sailing in the distance

The desserts lined up in the café display
The faces of strangers
The laughter of children
The statue's marble
The appraising eye
The sheet of music
The glorious shadows
The painted canvas
The burning ends of cigarettes
The value of kindness
The wisdom of humility
The beauty of integrity
The worth of dignity
The melody of language
The elegance of nature
The blue of the sea
The grey of stone
The black of night
The ones we smile at as we walk by
The ones who tuck their hair behind their ears
Stories not recorded
Photographs not taken
Exhausted words
Glorious failures
Rerouted dreams
Discarded plans
Unrepeatable moments
Gentle invitations
Advice not given
Promises unmet
Envelopes not stamped
Songs unsung
Imperfection
Impermanence
Silence
Solitude

And all the flowers fighting their way through cement.

About the Author

Stephan Silich has been writing poems and short stories for over thirty years. His first collection, 'the silence between what i think and what i say' was published in late 2018 by the Brooklyn Writers Press. Stephan is a native New Yorker and lives in Manhattan and East Hampton with his two daughters, Emma and Mia.

To find out more about his work and current projects, please visit:

www.brooklynwriterspress.com.
www.stephansilich.com

Connect with Stephan on Instagram: @stephan_silich

*Proceeds from the sales of Stephan's poetry collections will be donated to the Brooklyn Writers Press in an effort to support founder, Marina Aris' inspiring and brave mission of championing and publishing unknown and independent authors.

Thank you for reading
Tonight Will Be The Longest Night of Them All

If you enjoyed this book, please consider leaving
a short review on Goodreads or your website of choice.

Reviews help both readers and writers.
They are an easy way to support good work and
help to encourage the continued release of quality content.

Want the latest from the Brooklyn Writers Press?
Browse our complete catalog.
www.brooklynwriterspress.com

BROOKLYN
WRITERS PRESS

CPSIA information can be obtained
at www.ICGtesting.com
Printed in the USA
BVHW031913261120
594296BV00015B/104/J

9 781734 097344